LIVING WITH

INTENT

A JOURNAL THAT USES BOTH THE CONSCIOUS
AND THE SUBCONSCIOUS MIND

Michele Lee Nieves

It's been said that our external world is a manifestation of our inner world, what goes on in the confinements of our minds. Our thoughts lead to feelings, and our feelings either move us toward or away from our hopes, dreams, empowering beliefs and goals in life.

The bible tells us that the heart is the seed of motivation. Within our heart are our motives and feelings. Feelings are powerful – they can do one of two things: they either motivate us into action or they demotivate us into procrastination, even if that means we put off what we most need or want in life.

Our feelings are the driving force behind our actions – what we do and what we hold back from doing. And while our feelings are strong and relatively easy to notice – it's often the thoughts behind those feelings that are so inaudible in our minds that we barely hear what's being said – meanwhile we are left with overwhelming emotions that either drive us toward success or hold us back from even trying to get there.

Anything in our life that we find is unwanted, can be traced back to our actions or lack of actions. Behind those actions lie the feelings that are responsible for those actions or lack of actions. Peeling it back even further, we would find that beneath those feelings are the thoughts that are the driving force for those feelings.

When we realize the truth, when we truly grasp this reality – we conclude that the secret to everything that we have or don't have in our life, whether external things or internal empowering beliefs and high vibrational emotions, are all the result of our thoughts.

When we fail to grasp this truth, we go about trying to change our EXTERNAL reality thinking that this will result in the happiness, joy, confidence and success that we long for. However the external alone is not enough, so we wind up hitting road block after road block, stuck in a pattern of striving for a goal, beginning to see a small amount of change and then BAM our subconscious mind sabotages it since it is out of alignment with our inner reality and we are back to square one over and over again. We feel stuck in a loop with no way out.

We must come to grips with the fact that if there are things about our current reality that we do not like (whether they are external, internal things or both), the first step toward changing and improving our circumstances is NOT anything external that we need to do, rather it is internal – we must first change our mindset since this is the birthplace of the feelings that will govern and motivate our actions.

Some individuals attempt to improve their external circumstances and/or their internal outlook of themselves by utilizing affirmations and positive thinking.

For example, a person battling a lack of self-worth may attempt to say, "I am worthy," over and over again to override the limiting belief that they are not worthy.

While this may work for some people, for anyone that has undergone emotional abuse, narcissistic abuse or childhood trauma – positive affirmations feel as effective as using a spoon to get rid of the water that is sinking your boat in a storm.

The reason affirmations don't work is because our subconscious mind does not lie – ever! Nor will it accept a lie. The thought "I am worthy" may live and exist in the conscious mind through affirmations, but if we truly don't believe it due to our subconscious beliefs – it will never get through the door separating our conscious mind from our subconscious mind. The belief that lives in our subconscious mind will always be our true reality and the mind's job (other than to keep us alive) is to prove to us our own reality.

Think about a closet in your home. Let's say your closet if full – floor to ceiling – with old items you've had stored in there for decades, and now you have new items that you want to put into that closet. The problem is that there is no room for the new items. If you were to wish and tell yourself "I have room in that closet for new things" repeatedly – the reality is, you don't. Before placing anything new into that closet, you must first clear out the old to have the room.

Put simply – action is required first.

It's the same thing with our brain. Sometimes we must trick our brain into moving us in the direction we long to move toward. In order to do this, we must acknowledge that what we want in our closet (or our subconscious mind) is not currently there and we need to figure out how to get it in there.

Regarding limiting beliefs – we need to acknowledge that the beliefs that we want are currently not within us. When we trick the brain in this way, we prompt the subconscious mind to notice the reality that we truly want, and we show it a map of how to help us to bring about this new reality.

The technique used in this journal will give your subconscious mind the ability to see your desired empowering beliefs, the positive results of having those beliefs, what actions are needed to reach those beliefs while acknowledging the pain of the current limiting beliefs that have been affecting your reality.

While using this journaling method, you will be able to overcome rumination, live mindfully present, strengthen self-validation, increase self-love and learn how to generate a truly peaceful and happier self.

What's great about this technique is that it can be done in only 5 minutes a day!!!Utilizing this technique daily will help you to stop reacting to life and will help you to live with intent, in a way that motivates you toward a reality that you truly desire.

As a life coach I often use this method with my face to face clients through a use of questions that cause self-reflection and shine a light into the dark spots that are holding people back. The technique in this journal will also help you to learn how to coach yourself as well!!!

On most days it will take you only about 5 minutes to do the entry for the day. This may tempt you to go ahead – and do several each day. **I am going to encourage you to exercise self-control. The subconscious mind learns through habit – through our everyday small, daily, consistent actions.**

Enjoy the 5-minute journaling process – and rather than skip ahead – do it daily and you will get the most benefit!!!!

Rumination: is the focused attention on the symptoms of your distress, on it's possible causes and consequences as opposed to focusing on its solutions.

Anyone that has been through emotional manipulation or trauma due to emotional abuse, has battled rumination at one time or another. Not only does rumination cause you to be overly focused on symptoms but that focus is always tainted with negative self-talk as well as black and white thinking.

"I never say the right thing." "No matter how hard I try I can never make him/her happy – I'm such a failure." "My own parents hate me – there must be something wrong with me."

Ruminating keeps you dwelling on and amplifying the stressful and upsetting situations in your life without providing you with a solution, a way out, or any kind of relief for that matter. Unfortunately, our minds can stay stuck in mental loops that leave us feeling awful – when we feel awful, we have no desire to attempt anything or do anything to make our life happier. Our lack of acting, due to our feeling awful, which is being driven by rumination – depresses us and therefore causes us to strengthen the negative beliefs or *circumstances that we are ruminating about*.

Date: _____

What are some things that my mind obsesses about:

_____
_____
_____

_____

What are the positive things that come from ruminating about this:

_____

_____

What are the negative things that come from ruminating about this:

_____
_____
_____

_____

If I no longer ruminated about this how would I feel?

_____

_____

What do I need to know or believe in order to let go of ruminating about this?

_____
_____
_____
_____
_____

Date: _____

What are a couple of things that I do daily while stuck in my head, with my body in automatic pilot rather than living in the moment and enjoying it?

_____
_____

What would my life be like if I lived more inside of my body rather than up in my head? (Be as descriptive as possible utilizing all your senses)

_____
_____
_____
_____
_____
_____

What would I need to do in order to begin be more mindfully present?

_____
_____
_____

Date: _____

If I were to **guess** how many minutes or hours I spend stuck in obsessive thinking or worry – how much time do I average: _____
What would be a better way to spend those minutes/hours? (Be descriptive)

_____
_____
_____

How would changing the way I spend that time affect my overall emotions? (Be descriptive)

_____
_____

What beliefs prevent me from making this change?

_____
_____
_____

What beliefs do I need in order to make this change?

_____
_____
_____

Date: _____

When was the last time I ate a meal and was focused on the taste of the food, the feeling of being in the moment as opposed to stuck in my head? What was the meal?

_____

_____

When I am in my head as opposed to in my body, living in the moment – what feelings does this behavior create in me?

_____

_____

What feelings would I prefer to have within me?

_____

_____

Feelings follow thoughts; what thoughts do I need to have in order to create more positive emotions?

_____

_____

_____

_____

Sometimes we get disconnected from our gut instinct – gaslighting causes you to ask – "Did I do the right thing?" Is it wrong to be upset when someone ignores you?"
"If I do that for myself, am I a selfish person."

In order to strengthen the connection to self and end self-doubt – **intention is key.**

You must create the intention of hearing what your gut instinct is saying and then listening to and following what your gut instinct communicates. The more we take time to listen to our gut instinct and the more we follow through with what it tells us, the louder our inner voice, the more connected to self we feel and the more we trust ourselves without needing confirmation from others.

"The greatest weapon against stress is our ability to choose one thought over another." - William James

Date: _____

What decision in my life past or present, creates self-doubt in me?

_____
_____
_____
_____

How do I feel about this decision? What does my gut say about it?

_____
_____
_____
_____

What thoughts would I need to have in order to trust my gut instinct?

_____
_____
_____

How would my life change if I had those thoughts? (Be descriptive)

_____
_____
_____
_____
_____
_____

Date: _____

What limiting belief exists in me that I do not want in my life? (Pick one for now)

_____

What do I do (or not do) daily that keeps this belief alive? List as many as possible:

_____
_____
_____

If I changed this to a more empowering belief what would it be?

_____

What actions or thoughts would I need in order to have this belief within me? And how would that feel?
Be descriptive:

_____
_____
_____
_____
_____
_____
_____

Date: _____

One area where I would like to be able to trust myself has to do with:

_____

_____

_____

What would I need to believe and say to myself in order to see that I trusted myself regarding this situation?

_____

_____

_____

_____

_____

What prevents me from believing and saying these things to myself? Be specific

_____

_____

_____

_____

How would my life change if I trusted myself in this? Be as descriptive as possible:

_____

_____

_____

_____

_____

_____

_____

Date: _____

Today I have the intention of listening to my inner voice all day – I will try to be self-aware of the thoughts that go through my mind. I will also intentionally pay attention to how I respond to that inner voice – do I listen to it? Do I talk myself out of it? Do I doubt it? Do I trust it? Today's journaling can take place in the evening. Journal about what happened today, when you put this intention into action. Be descriptive and explain what you learned:

_____

_____

_____

_____

_____

_____

_____

_____

_____

_____

_____

_____

Date: _____

Where does my lack of trusting my gut instinct come from- Why DON'T I trust myself?

_____
_____
_____
_____

While I can't change the past, what can I do **today** that will strengthen my gut instinct:

_____
_____
_____

What would my life look like if I trusted my gut instinct? Be descriptive use all of your senses

_____
_____
_____
_____
_____
_____

What thoughts would I need to have in order to trust my gut instinct?

_____
_____
_____
_____

How would I feel about myself if I had those thoughts?

_____
_____
_____

ANYTHING YOU HAVE TO WORK HARD AT, PUT A LOT OF EFFORT INTO OR ANYTHING YOU HAVE TO STRUGGLE IN ORDER TO ACCOMPLISH – IS THE RESULT OF YOUR PROGRAMS NOT SUPPORTING THAT!! ANYTHING THAT COMES EASILY IS BECAUSE YOU HAVE A PROGRAM THAT ALLOWS THEM TO BE THERE.

Date: _____

What beliefs come easily to me?

_____
_____
_____

What do I want In my life (externally or internally) that is a struggle for me?

_____
_____
_____
_____

IF YOUR TROUBLES EXIST IN RELATIONSHIPS, FOR EXAMPLE, YOU KNOW YOU HAVE TO CHANGE YOUR BELIEFS ABOUT RELATIONSHIP. IF THEY HAVE TO DO WITH FINANCIAL SUCCESS – YOU KNOW YOU HAVE TO CHANGE YOUR BELIEFS ABOUT MONEY AND/OR SUCCESS.

What beliefs are keeping these struggles alive?

_____
_____
_____

What actions am I taking that prove that these beliefs are still deeply rooted within? What am I doing that proves the limiting beliefs are active and affecting me? List as many as possible.

_____
_____
_____
_____
_____
_____

Imagine what life would be like if I were free of these limiting beliefs. What would life look like? What would I be doing differently? Be specific, visualize and use all of your senses:

_____
_____
_____
_____
_____
_____
_____
_____
_____
_____
_____
_____
_____
_____
_____

Date: _____

What are some beliefs that I would like to have deep rooted in my subconscious mind?

_____
_____
_____
_____

If I already had these beliefs deep rooted in my subconscious – how would I act? Feel? What would be different in my life? Be specific, visualize and use all of your senses:

_____
_____
_____
_____
_____
_____
_____
_____
_____
_____
_____
_____

SPEND TIME THROUGHOUT THE DAY REMINISCING ABOUT THIS VISUALIZATION. FEEL IT, TASTE IT, SEE IT.

Date: _____

What are some things that my mind obsesses about:

_____
_____
_____
_____

What are the positive things that come from ruminating about this:

_____
_____

What are the negative things that come from ruminating about this:

_____
_____
_____
_____

If I no longer ruminated about this how would I feel?

_____
_____

What do I need to know or believe in order to let go of ruminating about this?

_____
_____
_____
_____
_____

Date: _____

What are some negative things I've said to myself this past week?

_____
_____
_____
_____

What feelings and actions do these thoughts generate in me?

_____
_____
_____
_____

What feelings and actions would I like to see in me?

_____
_____
_____
_____

What thoughts would I need to tell myself daily in order to see these feelings and actions in my life?

_____
_____
_____
_____

Date: _____

Today I am going to notice all the positive and good that exists within me. I am going to look for things I like about myself and I am going to take a moment to compliment myself for my good and I'm going to be kind to myself if I make a mistake. I am going to use my inner dialogue to talk to myself the way I talk to a dear and cherished friend. This evening I will journal about all the moments I had throughout the day where I complimented myself and how it felt to be focused on the good, how it felt to find it and validate it.

_____
_____
_____
_____
_____
_____
_____
_____
_____
_____
_____
_____
_____
_____
_____
_____

SOMETIMES WITHOUT REALIZING IT, WE HAVE INTERNALIZED THE VOICE OF SOMEONE THAT MISTREATED US. A TOXIC PARENT THAT CONSTANTLY SAID – "YOUR ARE BAD" "YOU ARE NOT GOOD ENOUGH" "YOU NEVER DO ANYTHING RIGHT" BECOMES" "I AM BAD" "I AM NOT GOOD ENOUGH" "I NEVER DO ANYTHING RIGHT". THE PROBLEM WITH THIS IS THAT AT SOME POINT YOU MAY REMOVE ALL TOXIC, HARMFUL INDIVIDUALS FROM YOUR LIFE – BUT IF YOU HAVE INTERNALIZED THEIR VOICE – THEY KEEP HARMING YOU…. EVEN IF THEY ARE THOUSANDS OF MILES AWAY AND YOU HAVE NOT SEEN THEM IN YEARS!!! WE MUST PHYSICALLY REMOVE TOXIC PEOPLE FROM OUR LIVES AND THEN WE MUST DO THE INNER WORK TO REMOVE THEIR POISONOUS IMPLANTED VOICE FROM WITHIN.

Date: _____

What are some toxic beliefs/thoughts that I may have internalized and made part of my inner dialogue?

_____
_____
_____
_____
_____

Why do I keep saying these things to myself?

_____
_____
_____
_____

What would happen if I no longer said these things to myself? How would my life change? Be specific

_____
_____
_____
_____
_____

What are some things I would need to do as well as some things I would need to be saying to myself in order to create this change?

_____
_____
_____
_____
_____

When these old, toxic beliefs or thoughts come into my mind, what can I do about it so as to not continue to internalize them? Strategize – be specific and detailed.

_____
_____
_____
_____
_____
_____
_____

Date: _____

What is one empowering belief that I would like to be part of my personal belief system today?

_____•_____

How would I be acting today if that truly was part of my personal beliefs?

_____

_____

_____

_____

What would I need to do today in order to make it part of my personal belief system?

_____

_____

_____

_____

_____

Today make it a goal to DO the things you just listed!!! Journal in the evening – how did it go?

_____

_____

_____

Date: _____

What external accomplishments do I love about myself?

_____

_____

_____

_____

What internal qualities and characteristics do I love about myself?

_____

_____

_____

_____

_____

I am worthy and enough because:

_____

_____

_____

_____

Today I will track how often I say something positive and upbuilding to myself!! Journal in evening, how did it go? What positive things do I say to myself:

_____

_____

_____

_____

_____

Date: _____

I tend to put the needs of others before my own – something that I would like to do for myself that I love, but often cannot find time for myself to do is:

_____

_____

How would that affect my life to love myself enough to make time for this? How would I feel? Be specific – include all our senses:

_____

_____

_____

_____

What would I need to believe and do in order to make sure to do this for myself?

_____

_____

_____

_____

_____

What would my inner dialogue need to say in order to be able to do this?

_____

_____

_____

_____

Date: _____

Why is it hard for me to make time for myself? What beliefs hold me back?

_____

_____

_____

_____

Are those beliefs true? Do I want them in my life?

_____

_____

What beliefs regarding loving myself and making time for myself do I want to have? If I had these beliefs – how would that change my life? Be specific.

_____

_____

_____

_____

What do I need in order for those beliefs to become my reality?

_____

_____

_____

_____

_____

_____

SOMETIMES WE REACT TO LIFE AS IF WE HAVE NO CHOICE IN THE MATTER. WE MAY THINK WE FEEL EMOTIONS DUE TO WHATEVER LIFE OR CIRCUMSTANCES ARE PROVOKING WITHIN US. WE FEEL THERE IS NO CHOICE WHEN IT COMES TO WHAT WE FEEL. HOWEVER, WE DO NOT HAVE TO REACT TO LIFE, WE DO NOT HAVE TO SIT BACK AND ALLOW LIFE TO GENERATE FEELINGS WITHIN US – <u>WE CAN TAKE AN ACTIVE ROLE IN OUR EMOTIONAL STATES, SIMPLY BY CHOOSING TO LIVE WITH INTENT.</u> IN THIS WAY, WE FACE THE SAME LIFE AND CIRCUMSTANCES THAT WE DO EVERY DAY – *BUT LIFE NO LONGER CONTROLS YOUR EMOTIONAL STATE – YOU DO!!* FOR THE NEXT FEW DAYS WE WILL SET A DAILY EMOTIONAL INTENT!!!

Date: _____

Today, the emotion or feeling that I would like to exhibit throughout the day – despite life or circumstances is:

_____

In order to exhibit that emotion or feeling – what does my inner dialogue need to sound like?

_____
_____
_____

If that is what I am telling myself – what emotions will that provoke within?

_____
_____

If those are my emotions – what actions will that create in me?

_____
_____
_____
_____

How will having this emotional state and this inner dialogue change my life?

_____
_____
_____

Date: _____

Today I want to feel inner joy. What will I need to do to feel joy throughout the day? Be specific:

_____
_____
_____
_____
_____
_____

In the evening journal – did I do what I needed to do in order to feel joy? How was it? What did I learn?

_____
_____
_____
_____
_____
_____
_____

Date: _____

Today, the emotion or feeling that I would like to exhibit throughout the day – despite life or circumstances is:

_____

In order to exhibit that emotion or feeling – what does my inner dialogue need to sound like?

_____
_____
_____

If that is what I am telling myself – what emotions will that provoke within?

_____
_____

If those are my emotions – what actions will that create in me?

_____
_____
_____
_____

How will having this emotional state and this inner dialogue change my life? Describe you're your life will be like in detail:

_____
_____
_____
_____
_____
_____

Date: _____

Today, despite the hardships and challenges in my life, I choose to feel grateful for the following reasons: (Come up with as many as possible)

_____
_____
_____
_____
_____
_____
_____
_____

Throughout the day – spend time reflecting on these things – in the evening journal – how did it feel to take time to notice what I am grateful for and spend time **feeling** that gratitude:

_____
_____
_____
_____
_____

Date: _____

Today I want to feel confident and comfortable in my own skin!! What do I need to believe about myself in order to accomplish this?

_____
_____
_____

What would I be doing or saying differently if I felt confident and comfortable in my own skin?

_____
_____
_____

How would I need to view the opinion of others in order to be confident and comfortable in my own skin?

_____
_____
_____

How would my life change if I were more confident and comfortable in my own skin? How do I feel about that? Be specific

_____
_____
_____
_____

Date: _____

Today, the emotion or feeling that I would like to exhibit throughout the day – despite life or circumstances, is:

_____

In order to exhibit that emotion or feeling – what does my inner dialogue need to sound like?

_____
_____
_____

If that is what I am telling myself – what emotions will that provoke within?

_____
_____

If those are my emotions – what actions will that create in me?

_____
_____
_____

How will having this emotional state and this inner dialogue change my life? Describe what your life will be like in detail:

_____
_____
_____
_____
_____

LOVING MYSELF AND TAKING CARE OF MYSELF SOMETIMES MEANS THAT I HAVE TO SAY **NO** TO OTHERS. SAYING NO TO OTHERS CAN BE UNCOMFORTABLE. SEEING OTHERS DISAPPOINTED AND UPSET CAN BE UNCOMFORTABLE AND IT CAN WAKE UP STRONG EMOTIONAL TRIGGERS. HOWEVER, SAYING NO IS ALSO A LOVING ACTION – IT SHOWS MYSELF THAT I LOVE MYSELF ENOUGH TO KNOW MY LIMITATIONS, I LOVE MYSELF ENOUGH TO NOT DO THINGS THAT CAUSE ME TO SACRIFICE MY OWN SELF LOVE AND SELF-RESPECT.

Date: _____

What are some things that I have difficulty saying no to?

_____
_____
_____
_____

What is my fear?

_____
_____
_____

When I don't say no and I give in so that others aren't upset, how does it make me feel inside?

_____
_____

What would happen if I began exercising my boundaries more and saying no when I needed to?

_____
_____
_____

Boundaries are not to make other people happy – boundaries are not for other people. Boundaries keep me safe; they keep me feeling connected to self. Sometimes people get angry when I put down a boundary – that's ok. They can respond and feel however they choose. I am not responsible for their emotional response. They are **allowed** to be disappointed and I am still allowed to uphold my boundary. What are some boundaries that I would like to begin enforcing?

_____
_____
_____
_____

If people get upset or angry regarding these boundaries, what do I need to believe in order to not give in and go against my own boundaries?

_____
_____
_____

If I start to feel uncomfortable when I see others upset, disappointed or angry – what does my inner dialogue need to sound like in order for me to stay grounded in my decisions?

_____
_____
_____
_____

Date: _____

What boundary(s) do I want to make sure to have in place today?

_____
_____
_____

What will I need to do in order to enforce this boundary?

_____
_____
_____

How would my life change for the better if I regularly enforced healthy boundaries? Be specific.

_____
_____
_____
_____
_____

Date: _____

What are some healthy boundaries that should exist in all relationships – emotional and physical boundaries? (If unclear, do a quick google search) Be specific

_____
_____
_____
_____
_____
_____
_____
_____
_____

We teach others how to treat us. Where do my boundaries need to be strengthened?

_____
_____
_____

What do I need to do, believe *and* say to myself in order to strengthen them?

_____
_____
_____
_____
_____
_____
_____
_____

WHEN WE WANT TO INCREASE SELF-LOVE -IT'S NOT ENOUGH TO SIMPLY SAY "I LOVE MYSELF NOW." ACTION IS REQUIRED. THINK ABOUT IT. IF YOUR SIGNIFICANT OTHER VERBALLY TOLD YOU THAT THEY LOVE YOU, YET THEY DO NOTHING **TO SHOW IT;** THEY NEVER HAVE TIME FOR YOU, PUT YOU LAST ALWAYS, DENY YOU WHAT MAKES YOU HAPPY BECAUSE THEY ARE TOO BUSY OR CONCERNED ABOUT THEMSELVES, SAY NO WHEN YOU WISH THEY WOULD SAY YES – WOULD YOU BELIEVE THEM? NO. THEREFORE WHEN WE TRY SELF-LOVE AFFIRMATIONS OUR SUBCONSCIOUS MIND REJECTS THE THOUGHT – *IT DOESN'T **BELIEVE IT** BECAUSE OF A LACK OF EVIDENCE.* JUST LIKE OUR LACK OF SELF-LOVE ACTIONS PROVE A LACK OF SELF-LOVE – THE OPPOSITE IS TRUE AS WELL: THE MORE EVIDENCE WE SEE OF SELF-LOVE IN OUR ACTIONS THE MORE IT GROWS WITHIN!!!!

Date: _____

What can I do today to show myself that I love myself?

_____
_____

What would I need to believe in order to do this?

_____
_____
_____

What would my inner dialogue need to sound like in order to accomplish this?

_____
_____
_____

How would I feel if I did this for myself today?

_____
_____

Date: _____

Something I can do today to show myself self-love is:

_____
_____

What would I need in order to make sure that I do this?

_____
_____
_____

How will it feel at the end of the day to look back and see that I accomplished this? Be specific – use all your senses.

_____
_____
_____
_____

How will my life change if I do this regularly? Be specific, use all you're your senses.

_____
_____
_____
_____
_____

Date: _____

Something that I used to love to do – that I stopped for whatever reason is:

_____

How did I feel when this was a part of my life?

_____

_____

Why did I stop?

_____

_____

What would I need to do(say or believe) in order to get back to this?

_____

_____

_____

How would I feel if I began doing this regularly once again? Be specific

_____

_____

_____

Date: _____

One small thing that I can do today to prove that I love myself is:

_____

Why would this make me feel loved by me?

_____

_____

How would doing this affect my day?

_____

_____

_____

What does my inner dialogue need to sound like in order to do this?

_____

_____

_____

_____

What do I need to believe about myself in order to do this?

_____

_____

_____

What limiting beliefs might make this difficult and what do I need in order to overturn them?

_____

_____

_____

_____

_____

_____

_____

ACTIONS OF LOVE ARE LIKE THE STITCHES OF A SWEATER – THE SWEATER DOES NOT STAY TOGETHER THANKS TO ONE OR TWO BIG STITCHES, BUT RATHER NUMEROUS, CONSISTENT LITTLE ONES. FOR OUR SELF-LOVE TO TRULY GROW AND BE A PART OF OUR EMPOWERING BELIEFS – IT'S NOT ENOUGH TO DO ONE OR TWO THINGS THAT SHOW SELF-LOVE, EVERY NOW AND THEN. BUT IT'S REALLY THE LITTLE, EVERYDAY THINGS WE DO. TAKING CARE OF OUR PHYSICAL APPEARANCE, EATING HEALTHY, TALKING KIND TO OURSELVES (HAVING A COMPASSIONATE INNER DIALOGUE), SETTING HEALTHY BOUNDARIES, ALLOWING YOURSELF TO ENJOY THE MOMENT, TASTING YOUR COFFEE AND FOOD AS OPPOSED TO BEING IN AUTO PILOT, ETC.

Date: _____

Today I will make a list of as many small things that I can do daily to show myself that I truly, deeply and compassionately love myself (list as many as possible):

_____
_____
_____
_____
_____
_____
_____
_____
_____
_____
_____
_____
_____
_____

If I were already doing these things daily, what would my life be like? What would my overall emotional wellbeing be like? Be specific and use all your senses – describe it as if it were already a reality:

_____
_____
_____
_____
_____
_____
_____
_____
_____
_____
_____
_____
_____
_____
_____
_____

BEFORE WE CAN BELIEVE IN A GOAL, WE FIRST MUST HAVE AN IDEA OF WHAT IT LOOKS LIKE.

VISUALIZATION IS A SIMPLE TECHNIQUE USED TO CREATE A MENTAL IMAGE OF A FUTURE EVENT. WHEN WE VISUALIZE OUR DESIRED OUTCOME, WE BEGIN TO "SEE" THE POSSIBILITY OF ACHIEVING IT. THROUGH VISUALIZATION, WE GIVE OUR SUBCONSCIOUS MIND A MAP TO OUR "PREFERRED FUTURE." WHEN THIS HAPPENS, WE ARE MOTIVATED AND PREPARED TO PURSUE OUR GOAL.

Date: _____

If I were already my authentic self, living life comfortable in my skin, being the 'me' that I know that I am inside, what are some of the things that I would be doing? Saying to myself? What would my life look like if I were connected to self, loving myself, happy with the person that I am? Be specific and use all your senses. Visualize it as if it were **already your reality!!**

_____
_____
_____
_____
_____
_____
_____
_____
_____
_____
_____
_____
_____
_____
_____
_____

What do I need (to do, think, say to myself or believe) in order to make this a reality?

_____
_____
_____
_____
_____
_____

What is stopping me from achieving this and how can I lift these roadblocks?

_____
_____
_____
_____
_____

Date: _____

What is something(s) that I have been putting off doing?

_____
_____

What beliefs keep me from moving forward and doing these things?

_____
_____

What belief do I need in order to stop putting these things off?

_____
_____

If I already had that belief how would that affect my life? What would I be doing? Visualize and describe as many details as possible:

_____
_____
_____
_____
_____
_____
_____
_____
_____
_____
_____
_____
_____

What does my inner dialogue need to sound like in order to strengthen this new and empowering belief?

_____
_____
_____
_____

ACCORDING TO RESEARCH USING BRAIN IMAGERY, VISUALIZATION WORKS BECAUSE NEURONS IN OUR BRAINS, INTERPRET IMAGERY THE EXACT SAME WAY AS THEY INTERPRET A REAL-LIFE ACTION. WHEN WE VISUALIZE AN ACT, THE BRAIN GENERATES AN IMPULSE THAT TELLS OUR NEURONS TO "PERFORM" THE MOVEMENT. THIS CREATES A NEW NEURAL PATHWAY THAT PRIMES US TO ACT IN A WAY CONSISTENT TO WHAT WE IMAGINED. ALL OF THIS OCCURS WITHOUT ACTUALLY PERFORMING THE PHYSICAL ACTIVITY, YET IT ACHIEVES A SIMILAR RESULT.

SEEING REALLY IS BELIEVING!!!!!

Date: _____

If I no longer needed external validation because my self-validation was strong and healthy – what would my life look like? What would change? How would this show up in my life? Visualize:

_____
_____
_____
_____
_____
_____
_____
_____
_____
_____
_____
_____
_____
_____

What are some areas in life where I want to strengthen my self-validation?

_____
_____

What would I need in order to do this?

_____
_____
_____
_____

Date: _____

What are some limiting beliefs that are affecting my happiness?

_____
_____
_____

What would my life look like if I were free of those limiting beliefs? Be specific – visualize & describe

_____
_____
_____
_____
_____
_____
_____
_____
_____
_____
_____
_____
_____

Date: _____

What kind of person do I want to show up as today? How do I want to feel? Be specific and descriptive:

_____
_____
_____
_____
_____
_____
_____
_____

What will my dominating emotion(s) be today?

_____

What do I need in order to be sure to do and feel these things ?

_____
_____
_____
_____
_____
_____
_____

Date: _____

If I truly had self-acceptance – how would I be acting? What would my inner dialogue sound like? What would I be doing differently? Visualize and describe:

_____
_____
_____
_____
_____
_____
_____
_____
_____
_____
_____
_____
_____
_____
_____
_____
_____
_____

 SPEND TIME THROUGHOUT THE DAY REFLECTING ON THIS VISUALIZATION AND HOW IT MAKES YOU FEEL!

WHEN WE HAVE THE NEED TO PLEASE OTHERS AT THE EXPENSE OF OURSELVES – WE ARE ESSENTIALLY SAYING: "I VALUE YOUR COMFORT OVER MY OWN. I VALUE YOU HAVING PEACE OF MIND OVER ME FEELING THAT I'M LIVING A LIFE OF AUTHENTICITY."

Date: _____

Where is people pleasing showing up in my life and affecting my happiness?

_____

_____

_____

If I overcame people pleasing – what would I be doing differently?

_____

_____

_____

_____

_____

What beliefs would enable me to do these things differently?

_____

_____

What would my inner dialogue need to sound like?

_____

_____

_____

Date: _____

What would my life look like if I was completely over the disease to please? Visualize & Describe:

_____

_____

_____

_____

_____

_____

_____

_____

_____

_____

_____

_____

_____

_____

_____

_____

_____

Date: _____

What are the pieces of myself that I hide from people that I don't know well?

_____
_____
_____

What beliefs cause me to hide these pieces of me?

_____
_____
_____

What beliefs would I need in order to be able to be me anywhere, anytime and with anyone?

_____
_____
_____

What would my inner dialogue sound like if I already had those beliefs?

_____
_____
_____

Date: _____

If I always showed up as my authentic self no matter who I was with, what would that look like? How would that feel? What would my life look like if I were doing this? What would I be doing differently? Visualize & describe using all of your senses:

_____
_____
_____
_____
_____
_____
_____
_____
_____
_____
_____
_____
_____
_____
_____
_____
_____
_____
_____
_____
_____

Date: _____

How does my negative inner critic affect me?

_____

_____

_____

How often do I say negative things to myself daily (guesstimate)? _____

Why do I say these negative things to myself?

_____

_____

What do I need in order to change my inner voice so that it is more compassionate and kind?

_____

_____

If I already had a healthy, compassionate inner dialogue – what are some things I would say to myself daily that would empower me to be my authentic self?

_____

_____

_____

How would my life change if I consistently spoke to myself in this manner? Be descriptive:

_____

_____

_____

_____

_____

Date: _____

Make a list of your best qualities and attributes. Challenge yourself – how many can you come up with?

_____

_____

_____

_____

_____

_____

_____

_____

_____

_____

_____

_____

_____

_____

_____

_____

_____

_____

_____

Date: _____

The fear of displeasing others is kept alive by what beliefs:

_____
_____
_____

Are these beliefs what I want inside of me? Why/Why not?

_____
_____
_____

What beliefs do I need to have in order to be me and be free of fear?

_____
_____

What would my inner dialogue need to sound like for this to happen?

_____
_____
_____
_____

Date: _____

Live with intent. Today I am going to practice being my authentic self. Rather than focusing on what I think s/he wants me to be, or how s/he is judging me – I am going to be checking in with myself. Asking myself - how do I feel? What do I need? What action do I really want to take? What can I say that would be authentic? My focus will be on how I SEE ME – NOT ON HOW OTHERS SEE ME. Right now, I will journal about how I can specifically do this today – this evening I will journal about how it went!

_____
_____
_____
_____
_____
_____
_____
_____
_____
_____

Did I live today with the intention of being my authentic self? How did it go? What did I learn?

_____
_____
_____
_____
_____
_____
_____
_____
_____
_____

ENERGY IS EMOTIONS IN MOTION. IF THE EMOTIONS IN MOTION IN YOUR BODY ARE LOW, YOU ARE DEPLETED, EXHAUSTED, BURNT-OUT, SLEEPLESS, ANXIOUS, DEPRESSED, NUMB

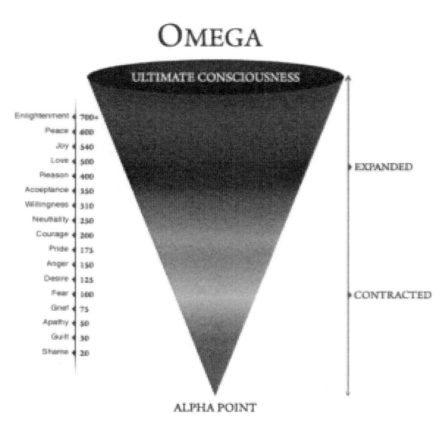

Shame and guilt have the lowest vibrations. Cancer radiates a low frequency or deficient energetic pattern in the body. The emotions involved in cancer are anger, grief, resentment, shame and guilt.

Date: _____

Do I have any toxic shame? (Toxic shame is an irrational feeling of worthlessness, feeling 'not good enough', self-loathing. It often comes from having a toxic person treat you in such a way that through repeated, traumatic experiences, toxic shame becomes hardwired into your psyche. Where does toxic shame show up in my life?

_____
_____
_____
_____

What would my life be like without toxic shame? How would It be different?

_____
_____
_____
_____
_____

Date: _____

When I feel shame – what are the thoughts that go through my mind?

_____
_____
_____
_____

To be free of shame – <u>what thoughts would I need</u> as part of my internal dialogue?

_____
_____
_____
_____

Live with intent. Throughout the day today – at what moments can I begin telling myself the things written above? Be descriptive – make it personal.

_____
_____
_____
_____

Date: _____

When I don't feel 'good enough' or valuable as a person – what are the things that I say to myself?

_____
_____
_____

If I imagined that at the moments I felt not good enough or valuable, were moments when my inner child was showing up in the present – revealing to me what s/he felt in the past– if I were to view it that way, would it change my inner dialogue? What would I want my inner dialogue to be? Be descriptive:

_____
_____
_____
_____
_____
_____
_____
_____

How would my life change if I spoke to myself this way? Be descriptive, use all of your senses:

_____
_____
_____
_____
_____
_____
_____
_____
_____

Date: _____

Live with intent. Today I am going to be aware of my inner dialogue. I realize that what I say to myself in the present – is also affecting my inner child and in essence I am saying those same things to him/her. Every time I catch myself saying something mean, critical, unkind, disempowering – I am going to ask myself – Would I say that to a small child? At that moment I will visualize what I looked like as a 5-year-old (or 8, 9-year-old, etc.) and I will ask myself – would I say this to him/her? If not – **What does s/he need to hear right now – and I will use my inner dialogue to give him/her what is needed**. Tonight, I will journal about how this went.

_____
_____
_____
_____
_____
_____
_____
_____
_____
_____
_____
_____
_____

Date: _____

What are some things I needed to hear as a child that no one ever told me? (As many as possible)

_____
_____
_____
_____
_____
_____
_____

Throughout the day – When and how can I go about telling myself these things?

_____
_____
_____
_____

If I were already doing this on a daily basis – how would my life be affected? Visualize – be descriptive:

_____
_____
_____
_____
_____
_____
_____

Date: _____

Live with intent. Today I am not going to reject my shame, I am going to validate it and give it the love it never had. When I feel shame in the present – I am truly connected to my inner child and s/he is revealing to me how much pain that shame created. I can heal that shame with love, validation and acceptance.

What will I say to shame when it shows up, so that it knows that I love and accept all the pieces of me?

_____

_____

_____

_____

_____

_____

You may think – I don't want to love my shame – I want it gone!! But – **what we resist persists**. The more we try to stamp out shame, reject and deny its existence the more powerfully it shows up in our lives. On top of that – is that how you really want to treat your inner child when s/he shows up?

THE OPPOSITE OF SHAME IS APPROVAL.

If I gave myself self-approval and acceptance – what would my inner dialogue sound like today?

_____

_____

_____

_____

_____

Date: _____

Live with intent. Today I am going to observe as many different feelings that come up. I will not judge my feelings as right or wrong – I will notice them and validate their existence. I will also ask myself what is behind this feeling? Why is it there. And with the curiosity of a child I will be the observer of my emotions today. In the evening I can journal what feelings came up and what I learned about them:

_____

_____

_____

_____

_____

_____

_____

_____

_____

_____

_____

_____

_____

_____

_____

Date: _____

What are some things, circumstances and/or people that make me feel guilty?

_____
_____
_____
_____

Putting the viewpoint of others aside, how do I want to feel about these things, circumstances?

_____
_____
_____

What do I need in order to stay grounded in my feelings, without allowing the perceptions of others to cause me to feel unnecessary and unhealthy guilt?

_____
_____
_____

What would my inner dialogue need to be?

_____
_____
_____

Date: _____

In my perception, what is the difference between selfish and self-love:

_____
_____
_____

What are things that I do that show I am selfish? Self-loving?

_____
_____
_____

If I do things that make me feel happy and others get upset, am I responsible for their feelings? If not – what do I need in order to be happy with loving myself even if others prefer that I focus on them alone?

_____
_____
_____

If I was already exercising healthy self-love, even if some people didn't want me to, what would my life look like?

_____
_____
_____
_____
_____
_____
_____
_____

Date: _____

What do I need to believe in order to let go of unhealthy and unnecessary guilt?

_____

_____

_____

If people try to make me feel guilty unnecessarily – what does my inner dialogue need to sound like in order to stay grounded within and not adopt their perception as my perception?

_____

_____

_____

_____

What would my life look like if I were free of unnecessary guilt? Be descriptive

_____

_____

_____

_____

_____

Date: _____

SOMETIMES WE FEEL GUILTY OVER THINGS WE FEEL WE HANDLED WRONG

Some things in the past that cause me to feel guilt are:

_____

_____

_____

_____

Regarding these past actions – if I truly forgave myself and displayed self-compassion for me…. How would this affect how I feel? How would it affect my life? Be descriptive & detailed.

_____

_____

_____

_____

_____

_____

_____

_____

_____

If I forgave myself and showed self-compassion – what would my inner dialogue sound like when these past actions come to mind?

_____

_____

_____

_____

_____

Date: _____

Why is forgiving myself for my past mistakes important?

_____
_____
_____

If I truly forgave myself for past mistakes – how would that be evident in my life?

_____
_____
_____
_____

If I had unconditional love for myself – what would my inner dialogue sound like when I made a mistake?

_____
_____
_____
_____

Date: _____

When I don't forgive myself or others, what emotions does a lack of forgiveness create in me?

_____
_____
_____
_____

If these emotions were a strong part of my daily existence – how would that affect me emotionally and/or physically?

_____
_____
_____
_____

If I were free of these emotions – what are some emotions that could be a dominant part of my day?

_____
_____
_____

What do I need in order to possess these more empowering emotions daily?

_____
_____
_____
_____

"FORGIVENESS IS THE DECISION AND THE ABILITY TO END THE NEGATIVE ENERGETIC CONNECTION THAT KEEPS ME LINKED TO THE PERSON OR PAST ACTIONS THAT HARMED ME. FORGIVENESS DOES NOT MEAN THAT I THINK WHAT THEY OR I DID WAS OK. RATHER, IT'S A DECISION NOT TO LET PAST HURT OR GUILT CONTINUE TO STAIN MY PRESENT AND OVERSHADOW MY FUTURE. IT'S NOT ABOUT THE PERSON – THAT I FORGIVE. WHETHER I FORGIVE ANOTHER OR MYSELF – IT'S ALWAYS ABOUT HEALING MYSELF. FORGIVENESS HEALS ME – AND I DESERVE THAT!"

Date: _____

What are some fears that I battle daily?

_____
_____
_____
_____

If I were free of these fears how would I be acting? What would I be doing differently?

_____
_____
_____
_____
_____
_____

What thoughts would empower me to be doing these things free of fear?

_____
_____
_____
_____

Date: _____

Today I choose to let go of things I cannot control such as:

_____
_____
_____

What thoughts cause me to worry and anxiety? List as many as possible:

_____
_____
_____
_____
_____
_____
_____

What thoughts would I need so as to let go of worry and anxiety? List as many as possible:

_____
_____
_____
_____
_____
_____
_____
_____
_____

Date: _____

What people or circumstances in my life create negative energy in me?

_____
_____
_____

What can I change? What can't I change?

_____
_____
_____

What do I need to believe and do in order to not soak up other people's negative energy?

_____
_____
_____
_____
_____
_____

Date: _____

NATURE HAS A VERY HIGH VIBRATION. BY SPENDING TIME OUTSIDE – WALKING BAREFOOT OR TOUCHING TREES, WE BECOME A PART OF A PROCESS CALLED "EARTHING." EARTHING ALLOWS OUR BODIES TO RECEIVE A CHARGE OF BENEFICIAL ENERGY FAST!

What is something I can do today so as to experience the benefit of earthing or grounding?

_____

What would I have to know and believe regarding grounding, in order to do this regularly?

_____
_____

What would my inner dialogue need to be in order to make grounding(earthing) a routine?

_____
_____
_____
_____

"AS YOU THINK ...YOU VIBRATE. AS YOU VIBRATE ...YOU ATTRACT." ABRAHAM HICKS

Date: _____

What thoughts keep me at a lower vibrational state, which generate emotions of shame, guilt, fear & anger? List as many as possible:

_____
_____
_____
_____
_____
_____

What thoughts would raise my vibrational state, which would generate emotions of peace, joy, love & passion? List as many as possible:

_____
_____
_____
_____
_____
_____
_____

If I already spoke to myself like this on a daily basis, how would I be acting? Feeling? Treating myself?

_____
_____
_____
_____
_____

Date: _____

The things I love about myself are: (List as many as possible – spend time reflecting on these things throughout the day)

_____
_____
_____
_____
_____
_____
_____
_____
_____
_____

Date: _____

What are some goals that I seem to always start and yet always seem to sabotage before ever fully reaching them consistently?

_____
_____
_____
_____
_____

What beliefs do I have that make it difficult to achieve these goals?

_____
_____
_____

What do I need to believe in order to end the sabotaging of these goals?

_____
_____

What does my inner dialogue have to sound like in order to believe?

_____
_____
_____

Date: _____

Today I am going to be self-aware and not only am I going to listen to the thoughts that go through my mind – but I am also going to actively look for opportunities to generate a positive, upbuilding and self-compassionate inner dialogue. I am going to challenge myself to see how many positive things I can say to myself today!! In the evening I am going to journal and write down the things I said, as well as how it felt to talk to myself in this manner all day.

_____
_____
_____
_____
_____
_____
_____
_____
_____
_____
_____
_____
_____
_____
_____
_____
_____
_____

ANYTHING YOU HAVE TO WORK HARD AT, PUT A LOT OF EFFORT INTO OR ANYTHING YOU HAVE TO STRUGGLE FOR TO MAKE IT HAPPEN – IS THE RESULT OF YOUR SUBCONSCIOUS PROGRAMS NOT SUPPORTING THAT!! ANYTHING THAT COMES EASILY IS BECAUSE YOU HAVE A PROGRAM THAT ALLOWS THEM TO BE THERE.

Date: _____

What comes easily to me?

_____
_____
_____

What do I want In my life (externally or internally) that is a struggle for me?

_____
_____
_____
_____

IF YOUR TROUBLES EXIST IN RELATIONSHIPS, FOR EXAMPLE, YOU KNOW YOU HAVE TO CHANGE YOUR BELIEFS ABOUT RELATIONSHIP. IF THEY HAVE TO DO WITH FINANCIAL SUCCESS – YOU KNOW YOU HAVE TO CHANGE YOUR BELIEFS ABOUT MONEY AND/OR SUCCESS.

What beliefs are keeping these struggles alive?

_____
_____
_____

What actions am I taking that prove that these beliefs are still deeply rooted within?

_____
_____
_____
_____

Imagine what life would be like if I were free of these limiting beliefs. What would life look like? What would I be doing differently? Be specific, visualize and use all of your senses:

_____
_____
_____
_____
_____
_____
_____
_____
_____
_____
_____
_____
_____
_____

Date:

What are some beliefs I would like to have deep rooted in my subconscious mind?

_____

_____

_____

_____

If I already had these beliefs deep rooted in my subconscious – how would I act? Feel? What would be different in my life? Be specific, visualize and use all of your senses:

_____

_____

_____

_____

_____

_____

_____

_____

_____

_____

_____

_____

SPEND TIME THROUGHOUT THE DAY REMINISCING ABOUT THIS VISUALIZATION. FEEL IT, TASTE IT, SEE IT.

Date: _____

What are some things that my mind obsesses about:

_____

_____

_____

_____

What are the positive things that come from ruminating about this?:

_____

_____

What are the negative things that come from ruminating about this?:

_____

_____

_____

_____

If I were to ruminate less today – when would I be intentionally aware?

_____

_____

If I let go of this rumination, what are some things I would have time to think about? How would thinking about these things change my day?

_____

_____

_____

_____

Date: _____

From the time I began this book, is there any point in the day that I used to live in automatic pilot, but now intentionally generate mindful awareness? If not – what can I do today to be mindfully present?

_____
_____

What would my life be like if I lived more inside my body rather than up in my head? (Be as descriptive as possible utilizing all your senses)

_____
_____
_____
_____
_____
_____

What would I need in order to begin being more mindfully present?

_____
_____
_____

Date: _____

If I were to **guess** how many minutes or hours I spend stuck in obsessive thinking or worry – how much time do I average? Is this number more or less than what I wrote at the beginning of this journal?

_____

What would be a better way to spend those minutes/hours? (Be descriptive)

_____
_____
_____

How would changing the way I spend that time affect my overall emotions? (Be descriptive)

_____
_____

What beliefs prevent me from making this change?

_____
_____
_____

What beliefs do I need in order to make this change?

_____
_____
_____
_____
_____

Date: _____

When was the last time I ate a meal and was focused on the taste of the food, the feeling of being in the moment as opposed to stuck in your head? What was the meal?

_____

_____

When I am living stuck in my head as opposed to in my body, living in the moment – what feelings does this behavior generate?

_____

_____

What feelings would I prefer to generate?

_____

_____

Feelings follow thoughts; what thoughts do I need to have in order to create more positive emotions?

_____

_____

_____

_____

_____

Date: _____

What decisions or actions in life, past or present, create self-doubt in me?

_____

_____

_____

_____

How do I want to feel about this topic?

_____

_____

_____

_____

What thoughts would I need to have in order to trust my gut instinct? List as many as possible

_____

_____

_____

_____

How would my life change if I had those thoughts? (Be descriptive)

_____

_____

_____

_____

_____

_____

_____

Date: _____

What limiting belief still exists in me that I do not want in my life? (Pick one for now)

_____

What do I do (or not do) daily that keeps this belief alive? List as many as possible:

_____
_____
_____
_____

If I changed this to a more empowering belief what would it be?

_____

What actions or thoughts would I need in order to have this belief within me? And how would that feel?
Be descriptive:

_____
_____
_____
_____
_____
_____
_____
_____
_____

Date: _____

Today, what is one area that I would like to trust my gut?

_____
_____
_____

What do I need to believe and say throughout the day, in order to see that I can trust myself regarding
this situation?

_____
_____
_____
_____
_____
_____

How would my life change if I trusted myself in this? Be descriptive.

_____
_____
_____
_____
_____
_____
_____
_____
_____

Date: _____

Today I have the intent of listening to my inner voice all day – being self-aware of the thoughts that go through my mind. I will intentionally pay attention to how I respond to that inner voice – do I listen to it? Talk myself out of it? Doubt it? Trust it? Today's journaling can take place in the evening. Journal about what happened today, when you put this intention into action. Be descriptive and explain what you learned:

_____
_____
_____
_____
_____
_____
_____
_____
_____
_____
_____
_____

Date: _____

Where does my lack of trusting my gut instinct come from- Why DON'T I trust myself? Is my self-trust getting a little stronger than it was a few months ago?

_____
_____
_____

While I can't change the past, what can I do **today** that will strengthen my gut instinct:

_____
_____
_____

If I already achieved the goal of trusting my gut – what would my life look like? Be descriptive use all of your senses:

_____
_____
_____
_____
_____

What thoughts would I need to have in order to trust my gut instinct?

_____
_____
_____
_____
_____

IN THE BEGINNING OF THIS JOURNAL YOU WROTE ABOUT LIMITING BELIEFS THAT YOU MAY HAVE INTERNALIZED DUE TO SOMEONE ELSE'S TOXIC TREATMENT. HOW ARE YOU DOING WITH THAT INTERNALIZED VOICE? IS IT STILL AS LOUD OR HAS IT GROWN SOFTER? OUR SUBCONSCIOUS MIND LEARNS BY HABIT. LET'S GO OVER THIS AGAIN:

Date: _____

What are some toxic beliefs/thoughts that I may have internalized and made part of my inner dialogue?

_____
_____
_____
_____
_____

Why do I keep saying these things to yourself?

_____
_____
_____

What would happen if I no longer said these things to myself? How would my life change? If I am still struggling – be as specific as possible. Visualize in as much detail as possible!

_____
_____
_____
_____
_____
_____

What are some things I would need to do as well as some things I would need to be saying to myself in order to create this change? What have I not applied or tried since I began this journal?

_____
_____
_____
_____
_____
_____

When these old, toxic beliefs or thoughts come into mind, what can I do about it so as to not continue to internalize them?

_____
_____
_____
_____
_____
_____

Date: _____

Today, what is one empowering belief that I would like to have as part of my personal belief system?

_____

How would my life change if that truly was part of my personal beliefs?

_____
_____
_____
_____

What daily actions would I need to take in order to make it part of my personal belief system?

_____
_____
_____
_____
_____

Today make it a goal to DO the things you just listed!!! Journal in the evening – how did it go?

_____
_____
_____

Date: _____

What external accomplishments do I love about myself?

_____
_____
_____
_____

What internal qualities and characteristics do I love about myself?

_____
_____
_____
_____

I am worthy and enough because:

_____
_____
_____
_____

Today I track how often I say something positive and upbuilding to myself!! Journal in evening, how did it go? What are the positive things I found myself saying to me??

_____
_____
_____
_____
_____

Date: _____

From the time I began this journal until now – has there been a change in where I place my needs as well as the needs of others? Explain:

_____
_____

If I valued my needs and were caring for them more now than when I began this journal – what are some small steps I would have already taken to begin this change? Name as many as possible. (How many are you doing?)

_____
_____
_____
_____

What beliefs are helping me to care about my needs? How does it feel to care for my needs and wants instead of putting them last?

_____
_____
_____
_____

What inner dialogue is helping me to make my needs more of a priority? If my needs are still not on my list of priorities – what is holding me back? How can I lift these roadblocks?

_____
_____
_____
_____

Date: _____

List some small ways I have been making time for myself. Are there still beliefs holding me back?

_____
_____
_____
_____

What evidence shows that those beliefs are true? Do I want those beliefs in my life?

_____

What beliefs regarding loving myself and making time for myself do I want to have? What is one small action I can begin doing today to make more time for myself?

_____
_____
_____
_____

If I already made time for myself daily – what would my life look like? Feel like? Be descriptive

_____
_____
_____
_____

Date: _____

Today, what is the emotion or feeling that I would like to exhibit throughout the day – despite life or circumstances?

_____

In order to exhibit that emotion or feeling – what does my inner dialogue need to sound like?

_____
_____
_____

If that is what I am telling myself – what emotions will that provoke within me?

_____
_____

If those are my emotions – what actions will result?

_____
_____
_____
_____

How will having this emotional state and this inner dialogue change my life? List as many changes as possible:

_____
_____
_____
_____
_____
_____
_____

Date: _____

What emotional state do I choose to have today? What will I need to do to feel this throughout the day? Be specific:

_____
_____
_____
_____
_____
_____

In the evening journal – did I do what was needed to generate my intended emotional state? How was it? What did I learn?

_____
_____
_____
_____
_____
_____
_____

Date: _____

Today, despite the hardships and challenges in life, what can I choose to feel grateful for? (Come up with as many as possible)

_____
_____
_____
_____
_____
_____
_____
_____
_____

Throughout the day – spend time reflecting on these things – in the evening journal – how did it feel to take time to focus on what I am grateful for and spend time **feeling** that gratitude:

_____
_____
_____
_____

Date: _____

Today I choose to feel _____!! What do I need to believe about myself in order to do this?

_____
_____

What would I need to do or say differently if I truly felt _____?
List as many things as possible:

_____
_____
_____

How would I need to view the opinion of others in order to feel _____?

_____
_____

How would my life change if I felt more _____? How do I feel about that? Be specific

_____
_____
_____
_____
_____
_____

SOMETIMES SAYING NO TO OTHERS AND ENFORCING BOUNDARIES AWAKENS FEAR. BUT THAT FEAR DOESN'T MAKE SENSE BECAUSE, IN ESSENCE, IT'S OK TO SAY NO, EVERYONE IS ALLOWED TO HAVE WANTS, NEEDS, DESIRES, LIMITATIONS, ETC. THE FEAR IS A CONDITIONED, IN-GRAINED FEAR FROM HAVING NEGATIVE CONSEQUENCES AS A CHILD WHEN SAYING NO OR TRYING TO ENFORCE BOUNDARIES. SO, BOUNDARIES TRIGGER THAT INNER WOUND FROM CHILDHOOD THAT OPENS THE DOOR TO THE FEAR FELT AS A CHILD. WHEN WE ARE TRIGGERED – THE LEFT SIDE OF OUR BRAIN SHUTS DOWN – WITHOUT THIS EXECUTIVE FUNCTIONING OUR MIND HAS DIFFICULTY DISCERNING BETWEEN PAST AND PRESENT. THE FEAR THAT WE FEEL IS OUT OF PROPORTION – IT'S THE FEAR THAT WAS FELT AS A CHILD.

Date: _____

When I say no or enforce boundaries what feelings come up? Where do they originate from?

_____
_____
_____
_____

Validate that fear by acknowledging why it's there – understand where it comes from and then ask yourself – what do I need in order to feel strong enough to continue to enforce healthy boundaries?

_____
_____
_____

Sometimes people are disappointed when we say no, sometimes they are upset or even angry. What do I need to know and believe in order to maintain my boundaries despite the disapproval from others?

_____
_____

How do I show that you respect the boundaries of others?

_____
_____
_____

Is it reasonable to expect others to show me the same respect? Why? How can I teach people to do this?

_____
_____
_____

If people get upset or angry regarding these boundaries, what do I need to believe in order to not give in and go against my own boundaries?

_____
_____
_____

If I start to feel uncomfortable when others are upset, disappointed or angry – what does my inner dialogue need to sound like in order to stay grounded in my decisions and boundaries?

_____
_____
_____

Date: _____

What boundary(s) do I want to make sure to have in place today?

_____
_____
_____

What will I need to do in order to enforce this boundary?

_____
_____
_____

How would my life change for the better if I regularly enforced healthy boundaries? Be specific.

_____
_____
_____
_____
_____
_____

Date: _____

What are some healthy boundaries that should exist in all relationships – emotional and physical boundaries? (If unclear, do a quick google search) Be specific. Circle all that do not exist in your relationships.

_____
_____
_____
_____
_____
_____
_____
_____
_____

We teach others how to treat us. What boundaries do I need strengthened?

_____
_____
_____

What do I need to do, believe *and* say to myself in order to strengthen them?

_____
_____
_____
_____
_____
_____

SELF-LOVE IS LIKE A MUSCLE. THE MORE WE EXERCISE THE STRONGER OUR MUSCLES AND THE MORE WE SEE THE PHYSICAL BENEFITS – THE MORE WE EXERCISE OUR SELF-LOVE THE MORE WE SEE THE EMOTIONAL BENEFITS. OUR SUBCONSCIOUS MIND LEARNS BY HABIT – IT'S NOT THE ONE OR TWO HUGE THINGS WE LEARN OR READ – RATHER IT'S THE EVERYDAY LITTLE THINGS WE DO FOR OURSELVES THAT STRENGTHEN THE SUBCONSCIOUS BELIEF THAT WE LOVE OURSELVES, THAT WE ARE VALUABLE IN OUR OWN EYES!!

Date: _____

What can I do today to prove to myself that I love myself?

_____
_____

What would I need to believe in order to do this?

_____
_____
_____

What would my inner dialogue need to sound like in order to accomplish this?

_____
_____
_____

If my self-love muscle was well worked and strong – how would my self-love change and shape my life – my outer world? My inner world? Visualize and be descriptive using all of your senses:

_____
_____
_____
_____
_____
_____
_____
_____
_____
_____
_____
_____
_____

"You cannot consistently perform in a manner which is inconsistent with the way you see yourself." – Zig Zaglar

Date: _____

Today I will show myself how much I love myself by:

_____
_____
_____

What would I need to say to myself (inner dialogue) in order to make sure that I do this?

_____
_____
_____

How will it feel at the end of the day to look back and see that I accomplished this? Be specific – use all your senses:

_____
_____
_____
_____

How will my life change if I do this regularly? Be specific, use all your senses:

_____
_____
_____
_____
_____

Date: _____

Have I stopped giving myself time to engage in things I was once passionate about? What is something I used to love – but stopped for whatever reason is:

_____

What would my life be like if I were engaging in this regularly in the present? (Describe how it would make you feel – not how it would make others feel!)

_____
_____

Why did I stop?

_____
_____

What would I need in order to get back to this? List as many things as possible:

_____
_____
_____
_____

What are some small steps that I can take to begin this once again? Break it down:

_____
_____
_____
_____

Date: _____

One small thing that I can do today to prove that I love myself is:

_____

Why would this make me feel self-love?

_____
_____

How would doing this affect my day? My mood?

_____
_____
_____

What does my inner dialogue need to sound like in order to do this?

_____
_____
_____
_____

What do I need to believe about myself in order to do this?

_____
_____
_____

What limiting beliefs might make this difficult and what do I need to do (say or believe) in order to overturn them?

_____
_____
_____
_____
_____
_____
_____

"I will not let anyone walk through my mind with their dirty feet." – Mahatma Gandhi

Date: _____

Here is a list of as many small things that I can do daily to show myself that I truly, deeply and unconditionally love myself (list as many as possible) How many do I do regularly?

_____
_____
_____
_____
_____
_____
_____
_____
_____
_____
_____

If I were already doing these things daily, what would my life be like? What would my overall emotional wellbeing be like? Be specific and use all your senses – describe it as if it were already a reality:

_____
_____
_____
_____
_____
_____
_____
_____
_____
_____
_____
_____
_____
_____
_____

OUR BRAIN DOES NOT DISTINGUISH BETWEEN REALITY AND IMAGINATION; THIS MEANS THAT WHAT YOU IMAGINE TO BE HAPPENING IS ACTUALLY HAPPENING AS FAR AS YOUR BRAIN IS CONCERNED!!

Date: _____

If I were already my authentic self, living life comfortable in my own skin, being the 'me' that I know I am inside, what are some of the things that I would be doing? Saying to myself? What would life look like if I were connected to self, loving myself, happy with the person that I am? Be specific and use all your senses. Visualize it as if it were already your reality!!

_____
_____
_____
_____
_____
_____
_____
_____
_____
_____
_____
_____
_____

What do I need (to do, think, say to myself or believe) in order to make this a reality?

_____
_____
_____
_____
_____
_____

What is stopping me from achieving this and how can I lift these roadblocks? Be specific:

_____
_____
_____
_____
_____
_____

Date: _____

What is something(s) that I have been putting off doing?

_____

_____

What beliefs keep me from moving forward and doing these things?

_____

_____

What belief do I need in order to stop putting these things off?

_____

_____

If I already had that belief how would that affect my life? What would I be doing? Visualize and describe as many details as possible:

_____

_____

_____

_____

_____

_____

_____

_____

_____

_____

_____

What does my inner dialogue need to sound like in order to strengthen this new and empowering belief?

_____

_____

_____

_____

SALLY GUNNELL IS AN OLYMPIC GOLD MEDALIST.

SHE EXPLAINED THAT WINNING THE GOLD WAS 70% MENTAL. AFTER FAILING TO WIN AT THE 1991 WORLD CHAMPIONSHIPS, SHE STARTED PRACTICING VISUALIZATION. SHE DID IT EVERY DAY, IMAGINING SPRINTING, HURDLING, AND EVEN HAVING THE STRENGTH TO HANG ON IN THE HOME STRAIGHT. THROUGH VISUALIZING IN THIS WAY, HER BRAIN WOULD HAVE UNDERGONE CHANGES THAT IMPROVED HER MUSCLES, GIVING HER BODY THE CAPACITY TO DO WHAT SHE HAD BEEN IMAGINING.

VISUALIZING WORKS!! BUT YOU DON'T HAVE TO TAKE MY WORD FOR IT – BEGIN PUTTING IT INTO PRACTICE – IT TAKES TIME SO BE PATIENT. PATIENCE PROTECTS YOU FROM BEING SO OVERLY FOCUSED ON THE DESTINATION THAT YOU DON'T ENJOY THE JOURNEY.

Date: _____

One goal that I have been striving to reach for a long time is:

_____
_____
_____

The limiting beliefs that keep this goal out of my reach are:

_____
_____
_____

Describe in detail what life will be like when I fully accomplish this goal:

_____
_____
_____
_____
_____
_____
_____
_____
_____
_____
_____
_____

Date: _____

If life was exactly how I wanted it to be – what would it look like. Describe everything – my external world, relationships, passions, inner dialogue, emotional state of mind, activities!!

_____
_____
_____
_____
_____
_____
_____
_____
_____
_____
_____
_____

Re-read what you just wrote- in order to accomplish this – what am I doing in the visualization that I am currently not doing in my life?

_____
_____
_____
_____

WHEN YOU ARE A SMALL CHILD COMPLETELY DEPENDENT ON YOUR CAREGIVERS –
REJECTION IS SYNONYMOUS WITH EXISTENTIAL DEATH. IF YOU HAD TOXIC PARENTS WHO
CONSTANTLY HURT, INVALIDATED AND REJECTED YOUR AUTHENTIC SELF EITHER OVERTLY
OR COVERTLY – YOU GREW UP INTO A WOUNDED AND SELF-LESS ADULT WITH AN OUT OF
FOCUS SELF-PERCEPTION. IF YOU NEVER UNDERSTAND THESE DYNAMICS AND WHY YOU ARE
SO DEPENDENT ON EXTERNAL VALIDATION – YOU RUN THE RISK OF BEING DEPENDENT ON
OTHER PEOPLE'S OPINIONS, JUDGMENTS, AND PERCEPTIONS OF YOU – WHICH SADLY, MAKES
YOU VULNERABLE TO MANIPULATION.

Date: _____

What were the negative messages that my caregiver caused me to feel?

_____
_____
_____
_____

What did I need my caregiver to tell me or help me to feel?

_____
_____
_____
_____

How can I help myself to feel that way? What can I say to myself to heal these wounds?

_____
_____
_____
_____

Date: _____

What are some limiting beliefs that are affecting my happiness?

_____
_____
_____

What would my life look like if I were free of those limiting beliefs? Be specific – visualize & describe:

_____
_____
_____
_____
_____
_____
_____
_____
_____
_____
_____
_____

Date: _____

If I had received the kind of unconditional love that I deserved as a child, what would my life be like now? What would my personality be like? Describe it as if it were your current reality:

_____
_____
_____
_____
_____
_____
_____

What do I do and/or say that reveals conditional love for myself?

_____
_____
_____

How can I begin to love myself unconditionally? List as many things as possible:

_____
_____
_____
_____
_____
_____

Date: _____

If I were to be 100% my authentic self – what emotions would I be feeling? How will I be acting? Be specific and descriptive:

_____
_____
_____
_____
_____
_____
_____

What do I need to do(say or believe) in order to be sure to experience this day the way I just described above? List as many things as possible – then strive to do them throughout the day.

_____
_____
_____
_____
_____
_____
_____

Date: _____

If I truly had self-acceptance – how would I be acting? What would my inner dialogue sound like? What would I be doing differently? Visualize and describe in as much detail as possible:

_____
_____
_____
_____
_____
_____
_____
_____
_____
_____
_____
_____
_____
_____
_____
_____
_____
_____
_____
_____

SPEND TIME THROUGHOUT THE DAY REFLECTING ON THIS VISUALIZATION AND HOW IT MAKES YOU FEEL!

In the evening journal: How did it feel to spend time in this visualization? What did I learn?

_____
_____
_____
_____
_____

How would my life change if I regularly spent time visualizing this? How would it affect me on a daily basis?

_____
_____
_____
_____
_____

WE NEED TO BE CAREFUL NOT TO CONFUSE RECEIVING APPROVAL OR VALIDATION FROM OTHERS WITH HAVING PERSONAL WORTH. IF WE BASE OUR VALUES AS A HUMAN ON OTHER'S APPROVAL, WE ARE TELLING OURSELVES THAT WE HAVE TO EARN SELF-WORTH AND VALUE. NO ONE OUTSIDE OF OUR SELF CAN GIVE INTRINSIC VALUE: ONLY WE CAN DECIDE WE HAVE IT. RATHER THAN RELYING ON EXTERNAL VALIDATION TO FULFILL OUR EMOTIONAL NEEDS – WE NEED TO ALLOW OURSELVES TO DO WHAT IS NEEDED TO FULFILL THOSE NEEDS!

Date: _____

Where is people pleasing still showing up in my life and affecting my happiness?

_____
_____
_____

If I truly believed that I didn't NEED anyone's approval, outside of my own, in order to feel good - what would I be doing differently throughout the day?

_____
_____
_____
_____

What would my internal dialogue sound like when I am validating myself?

_____
_____

Date: _____

Imagine that I have already conquered the need to please – while I enjoy making others happy, I have strong, healthy boundaries and put my own wants and needs at the same level. What does my life look if this were my reality? Visualize & Describe:

_____
_____
_____
_____
_____
_____
_____
_____
_____
_____
_____
_____
_____
_____
_____
_____
_____

Date: _____

What parts of my personality do I fear would get rejected?

_____
_____
_____

What beliefs cause me to hide these pieces of my authentic self?

_____
_____
_____

What beliefs would I need in order to be able to be me anywhere, anytime and with anyone?

_____
_____
_____

What would my inner dialogue sound like if I already had those beliefs?

_____
_____
_____

Date: _____

If I always showed up as my authentic self no matter who I was with, what would that look like? How would that feel? What would my life look like if I were already doing this? What would I be doing differently? Visualize & describe using all of your senses:

_____
_____
_____
_____
_____
_____
_____
_____
_____
_____
_____
_____
_____
_____
_____
_____
_____
_____
_____

Date: _____

Is my inner voice upbuilding or critical? What do I say to myself regularly that builds me up?
That tears me down?

_____

_____

_____

How often do I say negative things to myself daily (guesstimate)? _____
Why do I say these negative things to myself?

_____

_____

What do I need in order to change my inner voice so that it is more compassionate and kind?

_____

_____

If I already had a healthy, compassionate inner dialogue – what are some things I would say to myself
daily that would empower me to be my authentic self?

_____

_____

_____

How would my life change if I consistently spoke to myself in this manner? Be descriptive:

_____

_____

_____

_____

_____

Date: _____

Here is a list of my best qualities and attributes. Challenge yourself – how many can you come up with?

_____

_____

_____

_____

_____

_____

_____

_____

_____

_____

_____

_____

_____

_____

_____

_____

_____

Date: _____

The fear of displeasing others is kept alive by what beliefs:

_____
_____
_____

Are these beliefs what I want inside of you? Why/Why not?

_____
_____
_____

What beliefs do I need to have in order to be me and be free of fear?

_____
_____

What would my inner dialogue need to sound like for this to happen?

_____
_____
_____
_____

Date: _____

Live with intent. Today I will practice being my authentic self. Rather than focusing on what others want me to be, or how they are judging me – I will check in with myself. I will ask myself- how do I feel? What do I need? What action do I really want to take? What can I say that would be authentic? I will focus on how I SEE ME – NOT ON HOW OTHERS SEE ME. How can I go about specifically doing this today?

_____
_____
_____
_____
_____
_____
_____
_____
_____
_____

In the evening journal: Did I live today with the intention on being my authentic self? How did it go? What did I learn?

_____
_____
_____
_____
_____
_____
_____
_____
_____

TWO OF THE MOST IMPORTANT WORDS WE CAN USE TO CREATE THE LIFE WE WANT ARE: **I AM!!**

THOSE WORDS CONVEY OUR BELIEF SYSTEM REGARDING WHO WE ARE AND WHAT WE THINK WE SHOULD HAVE IN OUR LIVES. THE WORDS WE USE AFTER SAYING "I AM..." ARE EXTREMELY POWERFUL. HOWEVER, IF OUR FEELINGS AND OUR 'I AM' WORDS ARE NOT IN HARMONY – **THE FEELINGS WILL ALWAYS GOVERN AND DICTATE OUR LIFE.**

EXAMPLE: IF I **SAY** I AM ENOUGH – BUT I **FEEL** WORTHLESS .... I WILL CONTINUE TO ATTRACT AND BE ATTRACTED TO THINGS, PEOPLE, AND CIRCUMSTANCES THAT SUPPORT THE **FEELING** I AM WORTHLESS BECAUSE THAT BELIEF IS IN MY SUBCONSCIOUS PROGRAMMING!!!!

IF OUR FEELINGS OUR OUT OF HARMONY WITH OUR WORDS – IT'S IMPOSSIBLE TO IDENTIFY WITH THE POSITIVE BELIEF OR AFFIRMATION THAT WE ARE TRYING TO BUILD AND/OR STRENGTHEN.

HERE'S HOW WE CAN GET INTO THAT SUBCONSCIOUS PROGRAMMING SO THAT WE CAN USE AFFIRMATIONS TO HELP US CREATE THE LIFE WE TRULY WANT:
IN ORDER TO USE AN 'I AM' AFFIRMATION THAT WORKS – WE MUST TRULY BELIEVE IT AND FEEL IT!!

IF A BELIEF IS NEW AND NOT A PART OF OUR CURRENT REALITY, INSTEAD OF STARTING WITH I AM.... WE CAN ASK OURSELVES.... HOW AM I?

EX: HOW AM I ENOUGH?
WE CAN ASK THAT QUESTION AND THEN LISTEN TO WHAT COMES UP IN OUR MINDS:
I AM A GOOD PERSON. I HAVE A GOOD HEART. I AM KIND. I AM A CHILD OF GOD. MY CHILDREN LOVE ME. I AM A HARD WORKER. I'M A GOOD FRIEND. I'M GENEROUS.

ANOTHER EXAMPLE:
INSTEAD OF SAYING: 'I LOVE MYSELF" AND FEELING FULL OF SELF-HATE WE CAN SAY:

HOW AM I LOVING MYSELF?
I'M EATING HEALTHY. I AM CHANGING MY INNER DIALOGUE SO THAT I HAVE A MORE COMPASSIONATE INNER DIALOGUE. I GET READY FOR THE DAY (HAIR, MAKEUP, SHOWER, BRUSH TEETH) I HAVE REMOVED TOXIC PEOPLE FROM MY LIFE.
THE MORE YOU ASK YOURSELF THAT QUESTION THE MORE OF A MATCH YOU BECOME TO ANSWERS THAT SUPPORT THAT QUESTION THEREBY STRENGTHENING THAT BELIEF!

Date: _____

How am I exercising self-love? List as many ways (no matter how small) as possible:

_____
_____
_____
_____
_____
_____
_____
_____
_____
_____
_____
_____

Date: _____

How am I generating a spirit of gratitude daily? List as many ways (no matter how small) as possible:

_____
_____
_____
_____
_____
_____
_____
_____
_____
_____
_____
_____
_____

Date: _____

How am I trusting my gut instinct daily? List as many ways (no matter how small) as possible:

_____
_____
_____
_____
_____
_____
_____
_____
_____
_____
_____
_____

Date: _____

How am I generating happiness in my life? List as many ways (no matter how small) as possible:

_____
_____
_____
_____
_____
_____
_____
_____
_____
_____
_____

Date: _____

How am I generating peace in my life daily? List as many ways (no matter how small) as possible:

_____
_____
_____
_____
_____
_____
_____
_____
_____
_____
_____

Date: _____

How am I generating acceptance in my life daily? List as many ways (no matter how small) as possible:

_____
_____
_____
_____
_____
_____
_____
_____
_____
_____
_____

Date: _____

How am I learning to live in the moment? List as many ways (no matter how small) as possible:

_____
_____
_____
_____
_____
_____
_____
_____
_____
_____
_____
_____

Date: _____

How am I letting the past go and living in the now in my life daily? List as many ways (no matter how small) as possible:

_____
_____
_____
_____
_____
_____
_____
_____
_____
_____
_____
_____
_____

Date: _____

How am I displaying forgiveness to myself? List as many ways (no matter how small) as possible:

_____
_____
_____
_____
_____
_____
_____
_____
_____
_____
_____
_____

Date: _____

How am I living as my authentic self? List as many ways (no matter how small) as possible:

_____
_____
_____
_____
_____
_____
_____
_____
_____
_____
_____
_____

Date: _____

How am I generating positive beliefs in my life daily? List as many ways (no matter how small) as possible:

_____
_____
_____
_____
_____
_____
_____
_____
_____
_____
_____
_____

Date: _____

How am I kind to myself? List as many ways (no matter how small) as possible:

_____
_____
_____
_____
_____
_____
_____
_____
_____
_____
_____

Date: _____

How am I believing in myself? List as many ways (no matter how small) as possible:

_____
_____
_____
_____
_____
_____
_____
_____
_____
_____

Date: _____

How am I different today than I was when I was struggling within myself to love myself? List as many ways (no matter how small) as possible:

_____
_____
_____
_____
_____
_____
_____
_____
_____
_____
_____

Date: _____

How am I proud of myself? List as many ways (no matter how small) as possible:

_____
_____
_____
_____
_____
_____
_____
_____
_____
_____

Date: _____

How am I learning to live in the moment? List as many ways (no matter how small) as possible:

_____
_____
_____
_____
_____
_____
_____
_____
_____
_____
_____
_____

Date: _____

How am I letting the past go and living in the now in my life daily? List as many ways (no matter how small) as possible:

_____
_____
_____
_____
_____
_____
_____
_____
_____
_____
_____
_____
_____

Date: _____

How am displaying forgiveness to myself? List as many ways (no matter how small) as possible:

_____
_____
_____
_____
_____
_____
_____
_____
_____
_____
_____
_____

Date: _____

How am I learning to live in the moment? List as many ways (no matter how small) as possible:

_____
_____
_____
_____
_____
_____
_____
_____
_____
_____

Date: _____

How am I letting the past go and living in the now in my life daily? List as many ways (no matter how small) as possible:

_____
_____
_____
_____
_____
_____
_____
_____
_____
_____
_____

Date: _____

How am displaying forgiveness to myself? List as many ways (no matter how small) as possible:

_____
_____
_____
_____
_____
_____
_____
_____
_____
_____

Date: _____

How am I exercising self-love? List as many ways (no matter how small) as possible:

_____
_____
_____
_____
_____
_____
_____
_____
_____
_____
_____

Date: _____

How am I generating a spirit of gratitude daily? List as many ways (no matter how small) as possible:

_____
_____
_____
_____
_____
_____
_____
_____
_____
_____
_____
_____

Date: _____

How am I trusting my gut instinct daily? List as many ways (no matter how small) as possible:

_____
_____
_____
_____
_____
_____
_____
_____
_____
_____
_____
_____

Date: _____

How am I generating happiness in my life? List as many ways (no matter how small) as possible:

_____
_____
_____
_____
_____
_____
_____
_____
_____
_____
_____

Date: _____

How am I generating peace in my life daily? List as many ways (no matter how small) as possible:

_____
_____
_____
_____
_____
_____
_____
_____
_____
_____
_____
_____

Date: _____

How am I generating acceptance in my life daily? List as many ways (no matter how small) as possible:

_____
_____
_____
_____
_____
_____
_____
_____
_____
_____

Date: _____

How am I learning to live in the moment? List as many ways (no matter how small) as possible:

_____
_____
_____
_____
_____
_____
_____
_____
_____
_____
- -

Date: _____

How am I letting the past go and living in the now in my life daily? List as many ways (no matter how small) as possible:

_____
_____
_____
_____
_____
_____
_____
_____
_____
_____
_____
- -
- -

Date: _____

How am I displaying forgiveness to myself? List as many ways (no matter how small) as possible:

_____
_____
_____
_____
_____
_____
_____
_____
_____
_____
- -
- -

Date: _____

How am I living as my authentic self? List as many ways (no matter how small) as possible:

_____
_____
_____
_____
_____
_____
_____
_____
_____
_____
_____
- -

Date: _____

How am I generating positive beliefs in my life daily? List as many ways (no matter how small) as possible:

_____
_____
_____
_____
_____
_____
_____
_____
_____
_____
_____
_____
- -

Date: _____

How am I kind to myself? List as many ways (no matter how small) as possible:

_____
_____
_____
_____
_____
_____
_____
_____
_____
_____
- -

Date: _____

How am I believing in myself? List as many ways (no matter how small) as possible:

_____
_____
_____
_____
_____
_____
_____
_____
_____
_____
_____

Date: _____

How am I different today than I was when I was struggling within myself to love myself? List as many ways (no matter how small) as possible:

_____
_____
_____
_____
_____
_____
_____
_____
_____
_____
_____
_____
_____

Date: _____

How am I proud of myself? List as many ways (no matter how small) as possible:

_____
_____
_____
_____
_____
_____
_____
_____
_____
_____
_____
_____

Date: _____

How am I exercising self-love? List as many ways (no matter how small) as possible:

_____
_____
_____
_____
_____
_____
_____
_____
_____
_____
_____

Date: _____

How am I generating a spirit of gratitude daily? List as many ways (no matter how small) as possible:

_____
_____
_____
_____
_____
_____
_____
_____
_____
_____
_____
_____

Date: _____

How am I trusting my gut instinct daily? List as many ways (no matter how small) as possible:

_____
_____
_____
_____
_____
_____
_____
_____
_____
_____
_____

Date: _____

How am I generating happiness in my life? List as many ways (no matter how small) as possible:

_____
_____
_____
_____
_____
_____
_____
_____
_____
_____
_____

Date: _____

How am I generating peace in my life daily? List as many ways (no matter how small) as possible:

_____
_____
_____
_____
_____
_____
_____
_____
_____
_____
_____
_____

Date: _____

How am I generating acceptance in my life daily? List as many ways (no matter how small) as possible:

_____
_____
_____
_____
_____
_____
_____
_____
_____
_____
_____

Date: _____

How am I living as my authentic self? List as many ways (no matter how small) as possible:

_____
_____
_____
_____
_____
_____
_____
_____
_____
_____
_____

Date: _____

How am I generating positive beliefs in my life daily? List as many ways (no matter how small) as possible:

_____
_____
_____
_____
_____
_____
_____
_____
_____
_____
_____
_____
_____

Date: _____

How am I kind to myself? List as many ways (no matter how small) as possible:

_____
_____
_____
_____
_____
_____
_____
_____
_____
_____
_____
_____
_____

Date: _____

How am I believing in myself? List as many ways (no matter how small) as possible:

_____
_____
_____
_____
_____
_____
_____
_____
_____
_____
_____

Date: _____

How am I different today than I was when I was struggling within myself to love myself? List as many ways (no matter how small) as possible:

_____
_____
_____
_____
_____
_____
_____
_____
_____
_____
_____
_____
_____

Date: _____

How am I proud of myself? List as many ways (no matter how small) as possible:

_____
_____
_____
_____
_____
_____
_____
_____
_____
_____
_____
_____

Date: _____

How am I learning to live in the moment? List as many ways (no matter how small) as possible:

_____
_____
_____
_____
_____
_____
_____
_____
_____
_____
- -

Date: _____

How am I letting the past go and living in the now in my life daily? List as many ways (no matter how small) as possible:

_____
_____
_____
_____
_____
_____
_____
_____
_____
_____
_____
- -
- -

Date: _____

How am displaying forgiveness to myself? List as many ways (no matter how small) as possible:

_____
_____
_____
_____
_____
_____
_____
_____
_____
_____
_____
_____

Date: _____

How am I living as my authentic self? List as many ways (no matter how small) as possible:

_____
_____
_____
_____
_____
_____
_____
_____
_____
_____
_____
_____

Date: _____

How am I generating positive beliefs in my life daily? List as many ways (no matter how small) as possible:

_____
_____
_____
_____
_____
_____
_____
_____
_____
_____
_____
_____
_____

Date: _____

How am I kind to myself? List as many ways (no matter how small) as possible:

_____
_____
_____
_____
_____
_____
_____
_____
_____
_____
_____
_____

Date: _____

How am I exercising self-love? List as many ways (no matter how small) as possible:

_____
_____
_____
_____
_____
_____
_____
_____
_____
_____
_____

Date: _____

How am I generating a spirit of gratitude daily? List as many ways (no matter how small) as possible:

_____
_____
_____
_____
_____
_____
_____
_____
_____
_____
_____
_____

Date: _____

How am I trusting my gut instinct daily? List as many ways (no matter how small) as possible:

_____
_____
_____
_____
_____
_____
_____
_____
_____
_____
_____
_____

Date: _____

How am I generating happiness in my life? List as many ways (no matter how small) as possible:

_____
_____
_____
_____
_____
_____
_____
_____
_____
_____
_____
_____

Date: _____

How am I generating peace in my life daily? List as many ways (no matter how small) as possible:

_____
_____
_____
_____
_____
_____
_____
_____
_____
_____
_____
_____
_____

Date: _____

How am I generating acceptance in my life daily? List as many ways (no matter how small) as possible:

_____
_____
_____
_____
_____
_____
_____
_____
_____
_____
_____
_____
_____

Date: _____

How am I learning to live in the moment? List as many ways (no matter how small) as possible:

_____
_____
_____
_____
_____
_____
_____
_____
_____
_____
_____

Date: _____

How am I letting the past go and living in the now in my life daily? List as many ways (no matter how small) as possible:

_____
_____
_____
_____
_____
_____
_____
_____
_____
_____
_____

Date: _____

How am I displaying forgiveness to myself? List as many ways (no matter how small) as possible:

_____
_____
_____
_____
_____
_____
_____
_____
_____
_____
_____

Date: _____

How am I living as my authentic self? List as many ways (no matter how small) as possible:

_____
_____
_____
_____
_____
_____
_____
_____
_____
_____
_____
_____

Date: _____

How am I generating positive beliefs in my life daily? List as many ways (no matter how small) as possible:

_____
_____
_____
_____
_____
_____
_____
_____
_____
_____
_____
_____
_____
_____

Date: _____

How am I kind to myself? List as many ways (no matter how small) as possible:

_____
_____
_____
_____
_____
_____
_____
_____
_____
_____
_____
_____
_____
_____

Date: _____

How am I believing in myself? List as many ways (no matter how small) as possible:

_____
_____
_____
_____
_____
_____
_____
_____
_____
_____
_____
_____

Date: _____

How am I different today than I was when I was struggling within myself to love myself? List as many ways (no matter how small) as possible:

_____
_____
_____
_____
_____
_____
_____
_____
_____
_____
_____
_____
_____

Date: _____

How am I proud of myself? List as many ways (no matter how small) as possible:

_____
_____
_____
_____
_____
_____
_____
_____
_____
_____
_____
_____

How am I different today than when I began this journal? List as many ways (no matter how small) as possible:

_____
_____
_____
_____
_____
_____
_____
_____
_____
_____
_____
_____
_____
_____
_____
_____
_____
_____
_____
_____
_____
_____
_____
_____
_____
_____
_____
_____

"Be YOU - unapologetically!"
- Michele Lee Nieves

Gratitude is the act of feeling and communicating appreciation for the people, circumstances and material possessions in our lives. It allows us to cherish our present in ways that make us feel in abundance rather than deprived. As a result, we become more motivated, less fatigued and, ultimately, better off.

The positive effects of gratitude have been proven scientifically. In the book The Upward Spiral: Using Neuroscience to Reverse the Course of depression, One Small Change at a Time, talks about how gratitude boosts the neurotransmitters dopamine and serotonin and the hormone oxytocin; hormones that are associated with wellbeing and having a positive outlook on life. Deepok Chopra also writes about the clinical studies that have taken place and proven the positive effects of gratitude for those recovering from heart failure.

We know that focusing on what we dislike brings us down – we do not need to be neuroscientists to recognize this. Well, the opposite is true as well: when we focus on what we like, what makes us appreciative – it brings us up. Don't take my word for it – for the next 21 days practice strengthening your spirit of gratitude and measure how it helps your overall mood.

On a scale of 1 – 10 with 10 being super positive, energized, passionate and alive and 1 being no energy, negative inner critic, unable to find joy in life, unhappy – where are you? _____

Date: _____

3 Things I am grateful for today:

1. _____
2. _____
3. _____

Date: _____

3 Things I am grateful for today:

1. _____
2. _____
3. _____

Date: _____

3 Things I am grateful for today:

1. _____
2. _____
3. _____

Date: _____

3   Things I am grateful for today:

1. _____
2. _____
3. _____

Date: _____

3   Things I am grateful for today:

1. _____
2. _____
3. _____

Date: _____

3   Things I am grateful for today:

1._____
2._____
3._____

Date: _____

3   Things I am grateful for today:

1. _____
2. _____
3. _____

Date: _____

3   Things I am grateful for today:

1. _____
2. _____
3. _____

Date: _____

3 Things I am grateful for today:

4. _____
5. _____
6. _____

Date: _____

4   Things I am grateful for today:

4. _____
5. _____
6. _____

Date: _____

3   Things I am grateful for today:

4. _____
5. _____
6. _____

Date: _____

3   Things I am grateful for today:

1._____
2._____
3._____

Date: _____

3   Things I am grateful for today:

1. _____
2. _____
3. _____

Date: _____

3   Things I am grateful for today:
1. _____
2. _____
3. _____

Date: _____

3 Things I am grateful for today:

1. _____
2. _____
3. _____

Date: _____

3   Things I am grateful for today:

1. _____
2. _____
3. _____

Date: _____

3   Things I am grateful for today:

1. _____
2. _____
3. _____

Date: _____

3   Things I am grateful for today:

1._____
2._____
3._____

Date: _____

3   Things I am grateful for today:

1. _____
2. _____
3. _____

Date: _____

3   Things I am grateful for today:
1. _____
2. _____
3. _____

Date: _____

3 Things I am grateful for today:

1. _____
2. _____
3. _____

Date: _____

3   Things I am grateful for today:

1. _____
2. _____
3. _____

Date: _____

3   Things I am grateful for today:

1. _____
2. _____
3. _____

Date: _____

3   Things I am grateful for today:

1._____
2._____
3._____

Date: _____

3   Things I am grateful for today:

1. _____
2. _____
3. _____

Date: _____

3   Things I am grateful for today:
1. _____
2. _____
3. _____

Date: _____

3 Things I am grateful for today:

7. _____
8. _____
9. _____

Date: _____

5   Things I am grateful for today:

7. _____
8. _____
9. _____

Date: _____

4   Things I am grateful for today:

7. _____
8. _____
9. _____

Date: _____

4   Things I am grateful for today:

1._____
2._____
3._____

Date: _____

4   Things I am grateful for today:

1._____
2._____
3._____

Hope for a long life yet live every day as though it were your last. – Michele Lee Nieves

Made in United States
North Haven, CT
28 March 2023

34666169R00057